IMAGINE THE
ANGELS OF BREAD

W · W · NORTON & COMPANY · NEW YORK · LONDON

IMAGINE THE ANGELS OF BREAD

POEMS

Martín Espada

For information about permission to reproduce selections from this book, write
to Permissions, W. W. Norton & Company, Inc., 500 Fifth Avenue,
New York, NY 10110.

The text of this book is composed in Bodoni Book
with the display set in Poster Bodoni
Composition by Crane Typesetting Service, Inc.
Manufacturing by The Courier Companies, Inc.
Book design by Antonina Krass

Library of Congress Cataloging-in-Publication Data

Espada, Martín, 1957–
Imagine the angels of bread : poems / Martín Espada.
p.   cm.

1. Hispanic Americans—Poetry.   I. Title.
PS3555.S53I47   1996
811'.54—dc20   95-37926

ISBN: 978-0-393-31686-5

W. W. Norton & Company, Inc., 500 Fifth Avenue, New York, N.Y. 10110
http://www.wwnorton.com

W. W. Norton & Company Ltd., Castle House, 75/76 Wells Street, London W1T 3QT

7 8 9 0

This book is dedicated to the two Clementes:

Clemente Soto Vélez (1905–1993)
Clemente Gilbert-Espada (born December 28, 1991)

Contents

Acknowledgments
Imagine the Angels of Bread
Imagina los ángeles de pan

I

My Native Costume

II

Hands Without Irons Become Dragonflies

ACKNOWLEDGMENTS

Some of these poems have appeared or will appear in the following publications, to whose editors grateful acknowledgment is made:

Bilingual Review: "Huelga"; "Thieves of Light"; "My Native Costume"; "Sing in the Voice of a God Even Atheists Can Hear"; "Hands Without Irons Become Dragonflies"

Bloomsbury Review: "Cada puerco tiene su sabado"

Clockwatch Review: "The Man Who Beat Hemingway"

Crazyhorse: "The Trembling Puppet"; "The Hearse Driver"; "The Chair in the Dragon's Mouth"; "Soliloquy at Gunpoint"; "The Piñata Painted with a Face like Mine"

Fan: "The Fugitive Poets of Fenway Park"

Hanging Loose: "Beloved Spic"; "Governor Wilson of California Talks in His Sleep"

Indiana Review: "Because Clemente Means Merciful"; "The Sign in My Father's Hands"

Massachusetts Review: "Imagine the Angels of Bread"; "Do Not Put Dead Monkeys in the Freezer"

Mid-American Review: "The Owl and the Lightning"; "The Foreman's Wallet"

The Nation: "The Meaning of the Shovel"

North Dakota Quarterly: "The Good Liar Meets His Executioners"; "Thomas Jefferson and the Declaration of Food Stamps"

Parnassus: "Rain Delay: Toledo Mud Hens, July 8, 1994"

Partisan Review: "Public School 190, Brooklyn 1963"

Peregrine: "My Cockroach Lover"

Ploughshares: "Rednecks"; "Offerings to an Ulcerated God"

Poets & Writers: "My Twenty-Fifth Year Amazed the Astrologers"

Rethinking Marxism: "All the People Who Are Now Red Trees"; "Her Toolbox"; "When the Leather Is a Whip"; "Four Sandwiches"; "The Prisoners of Saint Lawrence"

The Progressive: "Sleeping on the Bus"

Tercer Milenio: "Hands Without Irons Become Dragonflies (bilingual)"

Threepenny Review: "The Bouncer's Confession"

Touching the Fire: Latino Poetry at the Turn of the Century: "My Native Costume"; "The Prisoners of Saint Lawrence"; "Do Not Put Dead Monkeys in the Freezer"; "Cada puerco tiene su sabado"; "Imagine the Angels of Bread"

"Imagine the Angels of Bread" was originally commissioned by National Public Radio, and broadcast on NPR's *All Things Considered* on January 2, 1994.

"Rednecks" and "Sleeping on the Bus" have been selected for *Best American Poetry* 1996 (Adrienne Rich, Guest Editor).

Many thanks to Jack Agüeros, Doug Anderson, Camilo Pérez-Bustillo, Cyrus Cassells, Katherine Gilbert-Espada, Angel Guadalupe, Paul Jenkins, Gary Keller, Demetria Martínez, Vilma Maldonado Reyes, Víctor Rivera, Earl Shorris, F. Joseph Spieler, and Marilyn Nelson Waniek for their support of this work.

IMAGINE THE
ANGELS OF BREAD

IMAGINE THE ANGELS OF BREAD

This is the year that squatters evict landlords,
gazing like admirals from the rail
of the roofdeck
or levitating hands in praise
of steam in the shower;
this is the year
that shawled refugees deport judges
who stare at the floor
and their swollen feet
as files are stamped
with their destination;
this is the year that police revolvers,
stove-hot, blister the fingers
of raging cops,
and nightsticks splinter
in their palms;
this is the year
that darkskinned men
lynched a century ago
return to sip coffee quietly
with the apologizing descendants
of their executioners.

This is the year that those
who swim the border's undertow
and shiver in boxcars
are greeted with trumpets and drums
at the first railroad crossing

IMAGINA LOS ANGELES DE PAN

Este es el año cuando los desamparados
echan a los terratenientes,
mirando como almirantes desde el barandal del balcón
o levantando manos en alabanza
del vapor de la regadera;
este es el año
cuando refugiados en rebozos deportan a los jueces
que miran fijamente al piso
y a sus pies hinchados
al ver sus expedientes estampados
con su destino;
este es el año cuando los revólveres de policía,
calientes como estufas, ampollan los dedos
de policias iracundos,
y sus macanas se hacen astillas
en la palma de sus manos;
este es el año
cuando hombres de piel oscura
linchados hace un siglo
vuelven para saborear calladamente un café
con la descendencia arrepentida
de sus verdugos.

Este es el año cuando los que nadan
la resaca de la frontera
y tiemblan en los furgones
son saludados por trompetas y tambores
en el primer cruce del ferrocarril

on the other side;
this is the year that the hands
pulling tomatoes from the vine
uproot the deed to the earth that sprouts the vine,
the hands canning tomatoes
are named in the will
that owns the bedlam of the cannery;
this is the year that the eyes
stinging from the poison that purifies toilets
awaken at last to the sight
of a rooster-loud hillside,
pilgrimage of immigrant birth;
this is the year that cockroaches
become extinct, that no doctor
finds a roach embedded
in the ear of an infant;
this is the year that the food stamps
of adolescent mothers
are auctioned like gold doubloons,
and no coin is given to buy machetes
for the next bouquet of severed heads
in coffee plantation country.

If the abolition of slave-manacles
began as a vision of hands without manacles,
then this is the year;
if the shutdown of extermination camps
began as imagination of a land
without barbed wire or the crematorium,
then this is the year;
if every rebellion begins with the idea
that conquerors on horseback

del otro lado;
este es el año cuando las manos
que cosechan los frutos de la tomatera
arrancan los títulos a la tierra que la hace brotar,
cuando las manos que enlatan tomates
son nombradas en el testamento
del dueño de la enlatadora caótica;
este es el año cuando los ojos
que arden por el veneno que purifica los inodoros
se despiertan por fin a la visión
de un monte lleno de gallos estrepitosos,
peregrinaje del nacimiento inmigrante;
este es el año de la extinción
de las cucarachas, cuando ningún médico
encuentra una enterrada
en el oído de un infante;
este es el año cuando los cupones de alimento
de madres adolescentes
se subastan como doblones de oro,
y no se da ninguna moneda para comprar machetes
para el próximo ramillete de cabezas decapitadas
entre los cafetales.

Si la abolición de los grilletes del esclavo
se inició con una visión de manos sin grilletes,
entonces este es el año;
si el cierre de los campamentos del exterminio
se inició con la imaginación de una tierra
sin alambre de púas y sin crematorio,
entonces este es el año;
si cada rebelión se inicia con la idea
de que los conquistadores a caballo

are not many-legged gods, that they too drown
if plunged in the river,
then this is the year.

So may every humiliated mouth,
teeth like desecrated headstones,
fill with the angels of bread.

no son dioses de piernas múltiples, que ellos también
se ahogan si son sumergidos en el río,
entonces este es el año.

Y que cada boca humillada,
sus dientes como lápidas profanadas,
se llene con los ángeles de pan.

Translation:
Camilo Pérez-Bustillo
and the author

1

My
Native
Costume

My grandfather slipped away
from the nursing home,
wandering through Brooklyn
and the year 1959,
till he found us.

This is from an age before understanding:
hunched and palsied, seeing me
for the first time,
he mounted a puppet
on his trembling hand,
and the puppet trembled looming
against my cheek. I screamed,
and the puppet faded away.

In the asylum
called King's Park Hospital,
he was the amnesiac
with spittle in the pockets
of his mouth.
Drink and disease left him
with a brain
the doctors would study
in a jar someday;
he did not know our names,
they said.
After the trembling puppet,
we did not see him again,

though my mother showed
the snapshot from 1930:
slick hair parted down the middle,
hands steady in the pose
of a bantamweight.

Fifteen years later,
the cancer telegram arrived,
and my mother rode
the commuter train
to the hospital.
When she opened the door
to his room, the man
without a memory said:
"Marilyn."

PUBLIC SCHOOL 190, BROOKLYN 1963

The inkwells had no ink.
The flag had 48 stars, four years
after Alaska and Hawaii.
There were vandalized blackboards
and chairs with three legs,
taped windows, retarded boys penned
in the basement.
Some of us stared in Spanish.
We windmilled punches
or hid in the closet to steal from coats
as the teacher drowsed, head bobbing.
We had the Dick and Jane books,
but someone filled in their faces
with a brown crayon.

When Kennedy was shot,
they hurried us onto buses,
not saying why,
saying only that
something bad had happened.
But we knew
something bad had happened,
knew that before
November 22, 1963.

THE SIGN IN MY FATHER'S HANDS

—for Frank Espada

The beer company
did not hire Blacks or Puerto Ricans,
so my father joined the picket line
at the Schaefer Beer Pavilion, New York World's Fair,
amid the crowds glaring with canine hostility.
But the cops brandished nightsticks
and handcuffs to protect the beer,
and my father disappeared.

In 1964, I had never tasted beer,
and no one told me about the picket signs
torn in two by the cops of brewery.
I knew what dead was: dead was a cat
overrun with parasites and dumped
in the hallway incinerator.
I knew my father was dead.
I went mute and filmy-eyed, the slow boy
who did not hear the question in school.
I sat studying his framed photograph
like a mirror, my darker face.

Days later, he appeared in the doorway
grinning with his gilded tooth.
Not dead, though I would come to learn
that sometimes Puerto Ricans die
in jail, with bruises no one can explain
swelling their eyes shut.
I would learn too that "boycott"

is not a boy's haircut,
that I could sketch a picket line
on the blank side of a leaflet.

That day my father returned
from the netherworld
easily as riding the elevator to apartment 14-F,
and the brewery cops could only watch
in drunken disappointment.
I searched my father's hands
for a sign of the miracle.

THE OWL AND THE LIGHTNING

—Brooklyn, New York

No pets in the projects,
the lease said,
and the contraband salamanders
shriveled on my pillow overnight.
I remember a Siamese cat, surefooted
I was told, who slipped from a window ledge
and became a red bundle
bulging in the arms of a janitor.

This was the law on the night
the owl was arrested.
He landed on the top floor,
through the open window
of apartment 14-E across the hall,
a solemn white bird bending the curtain rod.
In the cackling glow of the television,
his head swiveled, his eyes black.
The cops were called, and threw a horse blanket
over the owl, a bundle kicking.

Soon after, lightning jabbed the building,
hit apartment 14-E, scattering bricks from the roof
like beads from a broken necklace.
The sky blasted white, detonation of thunder.
Ten years old at the window, I knew then that God
was not the man in my mother's holy magazines,
touching fingertips to dying foreheads
with the half-smile of an athlete signing autographs.

God must be an owl, electricity
coursing through the hollow bones,
a white wing brushing the building.

—for Angel Guadalupe

"Cada puerco tiene su sabado,"
Guadalupe would say.
Every pig has his Saturday.

Guadalupe remembered a Saturday
in Puerto Rico, when his uncle Chungo
clanked a pipe across the skull of a shrieking pig,
wrestled the staggering blood-slick beast
before the flinching children.
Chungo set the carcass ablaze
to burn the bristles off the skin.
Guadalupe dreamt for years about
the flaming pig. Of his uncle,
he would only say:
"Cada puerco tiene su sabado."
And Chungo died, diving into the ocean,
an artery bursting in his head.

I remember a Saturday
on Long Island,
when my father dug a pit
for the pig roast,
and neighbors spoke prophecy
of dark invasion
beneath the growl of lawnmowers.
I delivered the suckling pig,
thirty pounds in my arms,
cradled in a plastic bag

with trotters protruding
and flies bouncing off the snout,
skinned by a farmer
who did not know
the crunch of cuero.
My father cursed the lost skin,
cursed the rain filling the pit,
cursed the oven too small for the pig,
cursed the pig he beheaded
on the kitchen counter,
cursed his friends who left
before the pig was brown.

Amid the dented beer cans
leaning back to back,
I stayed with my cursing father.
I was his accomplice;
witnesses in doorways saw me
carrying the body through the streets.
I ate the pig too,
jaw grinding thick pork
like an outfielder's tobacco.
The farmer told me
the pig's name: Ichabod.

Cada puerco tiene su sabado.

BELOVED SPIC

—Valley Stream, Long Island 1973

Here in the new white neighborhood,
the neighbors kept it pressed
inside dictionaries and Bibles
like a leaf, chewed it for digestion
after a heavy dinner,
laughed when it hopped
from their mouths like a secret,
whispered it as carefully as the answer
to a test question in school,
bellowed it in barrooms
when the alcohol
made them want to sing.

So I saw it
spraypainted on my locker and told no one,
found it scripted in the icing on a cake,
touched it stinging like the tooth slammed
into a faucet, so I kept my mouth closed,
pushed it away crusted on the coach's lip
with a spot of dried egg,
watched it spiral into the ear
of a disappointed girl who never sat beside me again,
heard it in my head when I punched a lamp,
mesmerized by the slash oozing
between my knuckles,
and it was beloved
until the day we staked our lawn
with a sign that read: For Sale.

THE PIÑATA PAINTED
WITH A FACE LIKE MINE

I was in the basement when my brother came home
without a shirt covering his hungry chest.
He saw a fight by the river,
eight-track tapes stolen from somebody's car,
a broken bottle jammed in the armpit
and blood shooting out, so that even my brother's shirt
wrapped around the wound
did not keep the startled boy from dying.
That summer my brother stayed by the river,
passing the lukewarm wine or a pipe of hashish,
bragging about refrigerators of meat
plundered in unguarded garages.

I saw him slip the bills from my father's wallet
into his pants. When I told my brother this,
he promised a kitchen knife
plunged between my ribs as I slept.
"Go get it," I said. When he turned
to the kitchen, a wave of blood crashed
in the chambers of my forehead.
Too quickly, my knuckles in his hair, his skull
thudding off the wall. I wanted to see
the blood irrigating the folds of his brain;
I wanted to break this piñata
painted with a face like mine.

Only amazement could have stopped me.
Amazing was the sight of my father's face.

He stood before us, a man with hands
forbidding as tarantulas, and cried.

After twenty years, one brother cannot sleep
waiting for the other. I wait for him,
the cool knife sliding against my skin.
And he waits for me, my knuckles in his hair,
to finish cracking open the piñata
painted with a face like mine.

REDNECKS

—Gaithersburg, Maryland

At Scot Gas, Darnestown Road,
the high school boys
pumping gas
would snicker at the rednecks.
Every Saturday night there was Earl,
puckering his liquor-smashed face
to announce that he was driving
across the bridge, a bridge spanning
only the whiskey river
that bubbled in his stomach.
Earl's car, one side crumpled like his nose,
would circle slowly around the pumps,
turn signal winking relentlessly.

Another pickup truck morning,
and rednecks. Loitering
in our red uniforms, we watched
as a pickup rumbled through.
We expected: "Fill it with no-lead, boy,
and gimme a cash ticket."
We expected the farmer with sideburns
and a pompadour.
We, with new diplomas framed
at home, never expected the woman.
Her face was a purple rubber mask
melting off her head, scars rippling down
where the fire seared her freak face,

leaving her a carnival where high school boys
paid a quarter to look, and look away.

No one took the pump. The farmer saw us standing
in our red uniforms, a regiment of illiterate conscripts.
Still watching us, he leaned across the seat of the truck
and kissed her. He kissed her
all over her happy ruined face, kissed her
as I pumped the gas and scraped the windshield
and measured the oil, he kept kissing her.

THE HEARSE DRIVER

One AM at Scot Gas
on Darnestown Road, and me
in a red uniform,
palms mapped with oil.
Sitting beside the other gas station boys,
I was debating God
and who would add the numbers
on the pumps, when a hearse
crawled up the driveway
and into the station.
Since I was the youngest,
and a boastful atheist, I was the one
who approached the driver.

The hearse driver:
a fedora too small for his head,
face round and glistening,
eyes sleepless-red,
a silver flask tipped into the funnel
formed by his lips.

I said no thank you to the flask.
"Which way's Richmond, Virginia?"
he wanted to know,
a hundred miles from here.
When I did not answer,
he told me that really was a casket
behind the curtains, son.

"Are you late?" I asked.
"I don't care," he said,
then nodded at the cargo: "*He* don't care."
I explained Richmond, Virginia,
as the hearse driver blinked and yawned.
"Turn right from here," I said, "and that's the highway."

He nodded again, wheeled the hearse around,
and turned left.

THE FOREMAN'S WALLET

At the printing plant,
I operated the machine
that shrink-wrapped paper
in clear plastic.
The bosses were Jehovah's Witnesses,
men pale as cheese
who sold Bibles door to door
on Sundays. They were polite,
and assembled the crew one night
to explain politely
that all of us were unemployed
by 11 PM.
No government contracts.
The plywood office door
pulled shut.

No one knows who set the first
wheel of paper rolling across the floor,
who speared the soda machine
with a two-by-four,
who winged unstapled copies of *Commander's Digest*
so they flew, with their diagrams of bombers,
through the room. Towers of legal pads collapsed,
fist-fired paper grenades hissed overhead.
A forklift truck without a driver bumped blindly
down the aisle, and we all saluted.
If we knew any songs, we would have sung them.

Saboteurs were unscrewing the punchclock
and rearranging the parts like paleontologists
toying with the backbone of a stegosaurus
when the foreman arrived,
his adolescent voice whining authority.
He was my last job.

The conspiracy to shrink-wrap
the foreman's head, turning red
in a wrestling hold, was a failure.
His skull was too big
to squeeze through the machine,
and even the radicals among us relented
when his eyes steamed with tears.
So we shrink-wrapped the foreman's wallet,
gleaming in the fresh plastic
like a pound of hamburger.

"Here's your wallet," I said. And mine.

Do Not Put Dead Monkeys in the Freezer

Monkeys at the laboratory,
monkeys doing countless somersaults
in every cage on the row,
monkeys gobbling Purina Monkey Chow
or Fruit Loops with nervous greedy paws,
monkeys pressing faces
through a grille of steel,
monkeys beating the bars
and showing fang,
monkeys and pink skin
where fur once was,
monkeys with numbers and letters
on bare stomachs,
monkeys clamped and injected, monkeys.

I was a lab coat and rubber gloves
hulking between the cages.
I sprayed down the batter of monkeyshit
coating the bars, fed infant formula in a bottle
to creatures with real fingers,
tested digital thermometers greased
in their asses, and carried boxes of monkeys
to the next experiment.
We gathered the Fear Data, keeping score
as a mechanical head
with blinking red bulbs for eyes
and a siren for a voice
scared monkeys who spun in circles,

chattering instructions
from their bewildered brains.

I did not ask for explanations,
even when I saw the sign
taped to the refrigerator that read:
Do Not Put Dead Monkeys in the Freezer.
I imagined the doctor who ordered the sign,
the moment when the freezer door
swung open on that other face,
and his heart muscle chattered like a monkey.

So I understood
when a monkey leapt from the cage
and bit my thumb through the rubber glove,
leaving a dollop of blood that gleamed
like icing on a cookie.
And I understood when one day, the doctors gone,
a monkey outside the bell curve of the Fear Data
shrieked in revolt, charging
the red-eyed mechanical head
as all the lab coats cheered.

I know about the Westerns
where stunt doubles bellyflop
through banisters rigged to collapse
or crash through chairs designed to splinter.
A few times the job was like that.
A bone fragment still floats
in my right ring finger
because the human skull
is harder than any fist.

Mostly, I stood watch at the door
and imagined their skulls
brimming with alcohol
like divers drowning in their own helmets.
Their heads would sag, shaking
to stay awake, elbows sliding out
across the bar.
I gathered their coats. I found their hats.
I rolled up their paper bags
full of sacred objects only I could see.
I interrogated them for an address,
a hometown. I called the cab,
I slung an arm across my shoulders
to walk them down the stairs.

One face still wakes me some mornings.
I remember black-frame eyeglasses
off-balance, his unwashed hair.

I remember the palsy that made claws
of his hands, that twisted his mouth
in the trembling parody of a kiss.
I remember the stack of books he read
beside the beer he would not stop drinking.
I remember his fainted face
pressed against the bar.
This time, I dragged a corkscrewed body
slowly down the stairs, hugged to my ribs,
his books in my other hand,
only to see the impatient taxi
pulling away. I yelled at acceleration smoke,
then fumbled the body with the books
back up the stairs, and called the cab again.

No movie barrooms. No tall stranger
shot the body spreadeagled across the broken table.
No hero, with a hero's uppercut, knocked them out,
not even me. I carried them out.

SOLILOQUY AT GUNPOINT

I sat in the car,
window down in summer,
waiting. Two boys
from the neighborhood
peered in the car
and did not recognize me,
so one opened his gym bag
and flourished a revolver
with black tape on the handle,
brushing the barrel's tiny mouth
against my forehead.

I sat calm as a burning monk.
The only god in my meditation
was the one who splices the ribbon of film:
a screen full of gunmen with sleepwalker's gaze,
confident detectives in silk neckties,
the cooing of hostage negotiators,
soliloquy at gunpoint
recited without stuttering.

I spread my hand
as if to offer salt
to a licking dog.
The script said, "Give me the gun,"
so I said, "Give me the gun."
And he did.

FOUR SANDWICHES

—Washington, D.C.

JC was called the Rack
at the work farm,
aluminum milk pails
dangling from his hands.
Once a sudden fist
crushed the cartilage of nose
across his face,
but JC only grinned,
and the man with the fist
stumbled away.

JC sings his work farm songs on the street,
swaying with black overcoat and guitar,
cigarettes cheaper than food.
But today he promises
four sandwiches, two for each of us.

The landlady, a Rumanian widow,
has nailed a death mask
over JC's bed,
sleeping plaster face
of a drowned girl
peaceful in the dark.

As the girl contemplates water
and pigeons batter the window,
JC spreads the last deviled ham
on two slices of bread,

presses them together,
then slowly tears four pieces.

"Here," he almost sings,
"four sandwiches."

The summer I slept
on JC's couch,
there were roaches
between the bristles
of my toothbrush,
roaches pouring
from the speakers
of the stereo.
A light flipped on
in the kitchen at night
revealed a Republican
National Convention
of roaches,
an Indianapolis 500
of roaches.

One night I dreamed
a giant roach
leaned over me,
brushing my face
with kind antennae
and whispering, "I love you."
I awoke slapping myself
and watched the darkness
for hours, because I realized
this was a dream
and so that meant
the cockroach
did not really love me.

My Twenty-Fifth Year
Amazed the Astrologers

My twenty-fifth year began in brilliant ice, January
Wisconsin sky frozen like a pond unbreakable over the drowned,
and me, hands in my coat, hunched at the welfare office
amid the congregation of scarecrows without a cornfield,
waiting for the check I would cash for half the rent
and three cans of chili. By April, I was the clerk periscopic
behind the desk of a welfare hotel, where a man hollering I love Go
plunged from the fifth floor, so I took a job at the Paterson Street
ballpark, licking the splintered grandstand with a broom.
June was Nicaragua, digging latrines, hearing bullets pop
in rum darkness, or a boy with the border patrol sing
the peasant mass, hands cradling the scarred brown belly of a guitar
Then I was home again, trapped in the window watching
two cops pin a suspect to the hood of a squad car
and club his body like blacksmiths at the forge,
and I did not dream the window brought me a mantis
shadowboxing on my pillow an hour later.
That same busted screen-door August, Felicia's cancer
bunched at the base of her throat like a bow tie, fingernails
painted red by her sister leaning over the coffin,
balloons streaming from the hearse.
In a month, I would drive a car with no muffler
through headlight-haunted truckstops before morning
from Chicago to D.C., then jump a train bellowing
against the night, solitary as whalesong from D.C. to Boston.
The catalog read: The School of Law, books with jaundiced pages
scrutinized in libraries for Latin incantations,
but I wore a lobster bib through the registration line

and Guadalupe led the gathering of our hands
in tumbao percussion, slapping the benches
in hallways of professors and judges who refused to dance.
So my twenty-fifth year amazed the astrologers,
the planets by Christmas zooming inebriated
inches away from a catastrophe of silence.

THOMAS JEFFERSON AND THE DECLARATION OF FOOD STAMPS

—Madison, Wisconsin 1982

I started with an emergency
food voucher, which I unraveled
like a Roman scroll at the grocery store.
I could hear the royal trumpets
behind me, and the customers
in the checkout line
cocked their heads, a row of curious dogs.

Then I got food stamps
from the Department of Agriculture,
with the Liberty Bell
on the cover of the booklet.
I opened my booklet of food stamps
to see Thomas Jefferson
and the Founding Fathers
signing the Declaration of Independence
on every one dollar coupon.
At the back of the booklet,
I found instructions on how to shop
and a warning that I could not buy
cigarettes or beer or restaurant meals
with food stamps.

I never smoked or drank
or ate in restaurants.
I only wanted what Jefferson said he wanted,

but the back of the booklet told me
I couldn't buy that with food stamps, either.

While waiting at the welfare office,
I would open my booklet of food stamps
and talk to Thomas Jefferson.
Were you the inventor of the food stamp?
Did you give food stamps to Sally Hemmings,
the slave with all the children
who looked like Thomas Jefferson?
I was a history major in college.

So I wrote my Declaration of Food Stamps:
proclaiming the right
to sit in a white linen restaurant,
eat as well as Thomas Jefferson,
then pay in piles
of clipped toenails
dumped into the tea.

THE MEANING OF THE SHOVEL

—Barrio René Cisneros
Managua, Nicaragua, June–July 1982

This was the dictator's land
before the revolution.
Now the dictator is exiled to necropolis,
his army brooding in camps on the border,
and the congregation of the landless
stipples the earth with a thousand shacks,
every weatherbeaten carpenter
planting a fistful of nails.

Here I dig latrines. I dig because last week
I saw a funeral in the streets of Managua,
the coffin swaddled in a red and black flag,
hoisted by a procession so silent
that even their feet seemed
to leave no sound on the gravel.
He was eighteen, with the border patrol,
when a sharpshooter from the dictator's army
took aim at the back of his head.

I dig because yesterday
I saw four walls of photographs:
the faces of volunteers
in high school uniforms
who taught campesinos to read,
bringing an alphabet
sandwiched in notebooks
to places where the mist never rises
from the trees. All dead,

by malaria or the greedy river
or the dictator's army
swarming the illiterate villages
like a sky full of corn-plundering birds.

I dig because today, in this barrio
without plumbing, I saw a woman
wearing a yellow dress
climb into a barrel of water
to wash herself and the dress
at the same time,
her cupped hands spilling.

I dig because today I stopped digging
to drink an orange soda. In a country
with no glass, the boy kept the treasured bottle
and poured the liquid into a plastic bag
full of ice, then poked a hole with a straw.

I dig because today my shovel
struck a clay bowl centuries old,
the art of ancient fingers
moist with this same earth,
perfect but for one crack in the lip.

I dig because I have hauled garbage
and pumped gas and cut paper
and sold encyclopedias door to door.
I dig, digging until the passport
in my back pocket saturates with dirt,
because here I work for nothing
and for everything.

THE CHAIR IN THE
DRAGON'S MOUTH

—Chelsea, Massachusetts

Once I worked in the kitchen at Ned's,
where every day I flattened
the dough of a hundred pizzas
refrigerated for weeks.
I scooped limp spaghetti
floating in a vat of ice water
and heated it under a faucet.
I was ordered to wash the walls
with dish detergent
for the Board of Health inspection.
I had a jukebox headache.

Fifteen years later, in Chelsea,
I stood below a rainstorm, blinking
at a drainpipe that gushed helplessly.
The 111 bus was stalled
by flooding like pneumonia in the sewer's lungs,
so I hid under my coat and ran
into Mystic House of Pizza.
I remember nothing about the woman
behind the counter
except a blond ponytail
and the glass of water she gave me
because I had no money,
while her husband rinsed dishes in the sink.
Together we waited till the green awning
of the pizza shop stopped dripping.

I returned on another day
when the buses could not pass.
Dropped off a block away,
I winced at kitchen smoke,
then saw the yellow warning tape
giftwrapping the street.
I stood before Mystic House of Pizza:
the burst ceiling dangling
its entrails, a chair upside down
through the window of jagged glass
jutting like teeth in a dragon's mouth.
The neighbors talked about
a greasy rag in flames, tossed
from the grill to the sink,
the fire jumping nimbly
to the garbage can, a hazy glow
blackening the room.
Later, I found a menu
from the pizza shop
folded in my coat.

The wrecking ball
pounded down half the buildings
on the block. There was rubble,
then earth, then the first grass,
rumors of a parking lot.
With the new seasons,
The neighbors stopped repeating
her words, what she said
to the weary firefighters about her husband:
Please don't tell him how it happened.
Please don't tell him it was me.

THIEVES OF LIGHT

—Chelsea, Massachusetts 1991

We all knew about Gus:
the locksmith, the Edison man, and me.
We heard about the welfare hotel,
where he stacked clothes
on the sidewalk for the garbage truck
if no rent was paid by Wednesday morning.
We heard about the triple deckers,
where he heaved
someone else's chair or television
from the third floor, and raged
like a drunk blaming his woman
till the pleading tenant agreed to leave.
There was word he even shot a cop
twenty years ago, but the jury
knew Gus too, studying cuticles
or the courtroom clock
as the foreman said not guilty.
The only constable in Chelsea
wore his gun in a shoulder holster,
drooped his cigarette at a dangerous angle,
yet claimed that Gus
could not be found on Broadway
to serve a summons in his hand.

This is how we knew Gus:
Luisa saw the sludge plop
from the faucet, the mice
dropping from the ceiling,

shook her head and said no rent,
still said no after his fist
buckled the bolted door.
In the basement, Gus hit switches.
The electric arteries in the walls
stopped pumping, stove cold,
heat off, light bulbs grey.
She lived three months in darkness,
the wax from her candle spreading
over the kitchen table like a calendar
of the constant night,
sleeping in her coat, a beggar
in the underworld kingdom of rodents.
When Luisa came to me, a lawyer
who knew Spanish,
she kept coughing
into her fist, apologizing
with every cough.

So three strangers
gathered in the hallway.
The locksmith
kneeled before the knob
on the basement door,
because I asked him
to be a burglar today.
The Edison man swallowed dryly,
because I asked him
to smuggle electricity today,
forget Gus's promise
of crushed fingers.
And me: the lawyer, tightly

rolling a court order in my hand
like a newspaper to swing at flies,
so far from the leatherbound books
of law school, the treatises
on the constitution
of some other country.

We worked quickly, thieves of light.
The door popped open,
as in a dream of welcome,
swaying with the locksmith's fingers.
The Edison man pressed his palms
against the fuse boxes
and awakened the sleeping wires
in the walls. I kept watch by the door,
then crept upstairs, past Gus's office
where shadows and voices
drove the blood in my wrist
still faster. I tapped on Luisa's door.
I had to see if the light was on.

She stared at me
as if the rosary
had brought me here
with this sudden glow from the ceiling,
a stove where rice and beans
could simmer, sleep without a coat.
I know there were no angels
swimming in that dim yellow globe,
but there was a light louder than Gus,
so much light
I had to close my eyes.

OFFERINGS TO AN
ULCERATED GOD

—Chelsea, Massachusetts

"Mrs. López refuses to pay rent,
and we want her out,"
the landlord's lawyer said,
tugging at his law school ring.
The judge called for an interpreter,
but all the interpreters were gone,
trafficking in Spanish
at the criminal session
on the second floor.

A volunteer stood up in the gallery.
Mrs. López showed the interpreter
a poker hand of snapshots,
the rat curled in a glue trap
next to the refrigerator,
the water frozen in the toilet,
a door without a doorknob
(No rent for this. I know the law
and I want to speak,
she whispered to the interpreter).

"Tell her she has to pay
and she has ten days to get out,"
the judge commanded, rose
so the rest of the courtroom rose
and left the bench. Suddenly
the courtroom clattered
with the end of business:

the clerk of the court
gathered her files
and the bailiff went to lunch.
Mrs. López stood before the bench,
still holding up her fan of snapshots
like an offering this ulcerated god
refused to taste,
while the interpreter
felt the burning
bubble in his throat
as he slowly turned to face her.

When you come to visit,
said a teacher
from the suburban school,
don't forget to wear
your native costume.

But I'm a lawyer,
I said.
My native costume
is a pinstriped suit.

You know, the teacher said,
a Puerto Rican costume.

Like a guayabera?
The shirt? I said.
But it's February.

The children want to see
a native costume,
the teacher said.

So I went
to the suburban school,
embroidered guayabera
short sleeved shirt
over a turtleneck,
and said, Look kids,
cultural adaptation.

HER TOOLBOX

—for Katherine Gilbert-Espada
Boston, Massachusetts

The city was new, so new
that she once bought
a set of knives
from the trunk of a car
and saw them rust
after the first rinsing.
She gathered with the tourists
at the marketplace of city souvenirs.
Still, she was the carpenter
for the community center
on Dorchester Avenue,
where men with baseball bats
chased the new immigrants
and even the liberals
rolled up their windows
at a red light.

The car on Dorchester Avenue
trailed behind her one night
as she walked to the subway.
The man talked to her
while he steered, kept taunting
when the car lurched
onto the sidewalk,
trapping her in a triangle
of brick and fender.
He knew her chest was throbbing;

that was the reason he throbbed too,
stepping from the car.

But the carpenter
unlocked her toolbox
and raised a hammer up
as if a nail protruded
from between his eyebrows,
ready to spike his balsawood forehead.
Oh, the hands like startled pigeons
flying across his face
as he backpedaled to the car
and rolled his window shut.

After the rusting discount knives,
the costly city souvenirs,
the men who gripped the bat
or the steering wheel
to keep from trembling,
she swung her toolbox walking
down Dorchester Avenue.

WHEN THE LEATHER IS A WHIP

At night,
with my wife
sitting on the bed,
I turn from her
to unbuckle
my belt
so she won't see
her father
unbuckling
his belt

BECAUSE CLEMENTE
MEANS MERCIFUL

—for Clemente Gilbert-Espada
February 1992

At three AM, we watched
the emergency room doctor
press a thumb against your cheekbone
to bleach your eye with light.
The spinal fluid was clear, drained
from the hole in your back,
but the X-ray film
grew a stain on the lung,
explained the seizing cough,
the wailing heat of fever:
pneumonia at the age
of six weeks, a bedside vigil.
Your mother slept beside you,
the stitches of birth still burning.

When I asked, "Will he be OK?"
no one would answer: "Yes."
I closed my eyes and dreamed
my father dead, naked on a steel table
as I turned away. In the dream,
when I looked again,
my father had become my son.

So the hospital kept us: the oxygen mask,
a frayed wire taped to your toe
for reading the blood,
the medication forgotten from shift to shift,
a doctor bickering with radiology over the film,

the bald girl with a cancerous rib removed,
the pediatrician who never called, the yawning intern,
the hospital roommate's father
from Guatemala, ignored by the doctors
as if he had picked their morning coffee,
the checkmarks and initials at five AM,
the pages of forms flipping like a deck of cards,
recordkeeping for the records office,
the lawyers and the morgue.

One day, while the laundry
in the basement hissed white sheets,
and sheets of paper documented dwindling breath,
you spat mucus, gulped air, and lived.
We listened to the bassoon of your lungs,
the cadenza of the next century, resonate.
The Guatemalan father
did not need a stethoscope to hear
the breathing, and he grinned.
I grinned too, and because Clemente
means merciful, stood beside the Guatemalteco,
repeating in Spanish everything
that was not said to him.

I know someday you'll stand beside
the Guatemalan fathers,
speak in the tongue
of all the shunned faces,
breathe in a music
we have never heard, and live
by the meaning of your name.

THE PRISONERS OF
SAINT LAWRENCE

—Riverview Correctional Facility,
Ogdensburg, New York 1993

Snow astonishing their hammered faces,
the prisoners of Saint Lawrence, island men,
remember in Spanish the island places.

The Saint Lawrence River churns white into Canada, races
past barbed walls. Immigrants from a dark sea find oceanic
snow astonishing. Their hammered faces

harden in city jails and courthouses, indigent cases
telling translators, public defenders what they
remember in Spanish. The island places,

banana leaf and nervous chickens, graces
gone in this amnesia of snow, stinging cocaine
snow, astonishing their hammered faces.

There is snow in the silence of the visiting room, spaces
like snow in the paper of their poems and letters, that
remember in Spanish the island places.

So the law speaks of cocaine, grams and traces,
as the prisoners of Saint Lawrence, island men,
snow astonishing their hammered faces,
remember in Spanish the island places.

THE MAN WHO BEAT HEMINGWAY

—for Kermit Forbes
Key West, Florida 1994

In 1937, Robert Johnson
still sang the Walking Blues,
the insistent churchbell of his guitar,
the moaning congregation of his voice,
a year before the strychnine flavored
his whiskey.

In the time of Robert Johnson,
you called yourself Battling Geech,
135 pounds, the ball of your bicep rolling
when you sickled the left hook
from a crouch, elbows blocking
hammers to the ribcage.
Florida for a Black man
was Robert Johnson, moaning:
the signs that would not feed you
hand-lettered in diner windows,
the motels that kept all beds white.

Here, in a ring rigged behind the mansion,
next to the first swimming pool
in Key West, you sparred with Hemingway.
He was 260 pounds in 1937, thick arms
lunging for you, so you slid crablike
beneath him, your shaven head
spotlit with sweat against his chest.
Only once did his leather fist tumble you,

sprawling across canvas
white as sun.

Now, nearing eighty, one eye stolen
from the socket, one gold tooth
anchored to your jaw,
you awoke this morning
and weighed the hurricane-heavy air
of Key West in your fighter's hands,
three decades after Papa Hemingway
choked himself with a shotgun.
You should stand before the mansion
on Whitehead Street, telling the amazed tourists
that you are the man who beat Hemingway,
and it happened here,
even if the plaque
leaves out your name.

Despite the rumors of rain,
the crowd spreads across the grandstand,
a hand-sewn quilt, red and yellow shirts,
blue caps. The ballgame is the county fair
in a season of drought, the carnival
in a town of boarded factories,
so they sing the anthem as if ready
for the next foreign war.
Billboards in the outfield
sell lumber, crayons, newspapers,
oldies radio, three kinds of beer.

The ballplayers waiting for the pitch:
the catcher coiled beneath the umpire's alert leaning;
the infielders stalking with poised hands;
then the pitcher, a weathervane spinning in wind;
clear echo of the wood, a ground ball,
throw, applause. The first baseman
shouts advice in Spanish to the pitcher,
and the pitcher nods.

The grandstand celebrates
with the team mascot
prancing pantomime in a duck suit,
a lightning bug called Louie
cheerleading for the electric company.
Men in Caterpillar tractor hats

rise from seats to yell at Louie
about their electric bills.

Ballpark lit in the iron-clouded storm,
a ghost dirigible floating overhead
and a hundred moons misting in the grey air.
A train howls in the cornfields.
When the water strikes down,
white uniforms retreat from the diamond,
but in the stands
farm boys with dripping hair
holler their hosannas to the rain.

II

Hands

Without

Irons

Become

Dragonflies

ALL THE PEOPLE WHO
ARE NOW RED TREES

When I see the red maple,
I think of a shoemaker
and a fish peddler
red as the leaves,
electrocuted by the state
of Massachusetts.

When I see the red maple,
I think of flamboyán's red flower,
two poets like flamboyán
chained at the wrist
for visions of San Juan Bay
without Navy gunboats.

When I see the flamboyán,
I think of my grandmother
and her name, Catalán for red,
a war in Spain
and nameless laborers
marching with broken rifles.

When I see my grandmother
and her name, Catalán for red,
I think of union organizers
in graves without headstones,
feeding the roots
of red trees.

When I stand on a mountain,
I can see the red trees of a century,
I think red leaves are the hands
of condemned anarchists, red flowers
the eyes and mouths of poets in chains,
red wreaths in the treetops to remember,

I see them raising branches
like broken rifles, all the people
who are now red trees.

How we drift in the twilight of bus stations,
how we shrink in overcoats as we sit,
how we wait for the loudspeaker
to tell us when the bus is leaving,
how we bang on soda machines
for lost silver, how bewildered we are
at the vision of our own faces
in white-lit bathroom mirrors.

How we forget the bus stations of Alabama,
Birmingham to Montgomery,
how the Freedom Riders were abandoned
to the beckoning mob, how afterwards
their faces were tender and lopsided as spoiled fruit,
fingers searching the mouth for lost teeth,
and how the riders, descendants
of Africa and Europe both, kept riding
even as the mob with pleading hands wept fiercely
for the ancient laws of segregation.

How we forget Biloxi, Mississippi, a decade before,
where no witnesses spoke to cameras,
how a brown man in Army uniform
was pulled from the bus by police
when he sneered at the custom of the back seat,
how the magistrate proclaimed a week in jail
and went back to bed with a shot of whiskey,
how the brownskinned soldier could not sleep

as he listened for the prowling of his jailers,
the muttering and cardplaying of the hangmen
they might become.
His name is not in the index;
he did not tell his family for years.
How he told me, and still I forget.

How we doze upright on buses,
how the night overtakes us
in the babble of headphones,
how the singing and clapping
of another generation
fade like distant radio
as we ride, forehead
heavy on the window,
how we sleep, how we sleep.

THE FUGITIVE POETS
OF FENWAY PARK

—Boston, MA 1948

The Chilean secret police
searched everywhere
for the poet Neruda: in the dark shafts
of mines, in the boxcars of railroad yards,
in the sewers of Santiago.
The government intended to confiscate his mouth
and extract the poems one by one like bad teeth.
But the mines and boxcars and sewers were empty.

I know where he was.
Neruda was at Fenway Park,
burly and bearded in a flat black cap, hidden
in the kaleidoscope of the bleachers.
He sat quietly chomping a hot dog
when Ted Williams walked to the diamond,
slender as my father remembers him,
squinting at the pitcher, bat swaying like a memory of trees.

The stroke was a pendulum of long muscle and wood,
Ted's face tilted up, the home run
zooming into the right field grandstand.
Then the crowd stood together, cheering
for this blasphemer of newsprint, the heretic
who would not tip his cap as he toed home plate
or grin like a war hero at the sportswriters
surrounding his locker for a quote.

The fugitive poet could not keep silent,
standing on his seat to declaim the ode
erupted in crowd-bewildering Spanish from his mouth:

"Praise Ted Williams, raising his sword
cut from the ash tree, the ball
a white planet glowing in the atmosphere
of the right field grandstand!

Praise the Wall rising
like a great green wave
from the green sea of the outfield!

Praise the hot dog, pink meat,
pork snouts, sawdust, mouse feces,
human hair, plugging our intestines,
yet baptized joyfully with mustard!

Praise the wobbling drunk, seasick beer
in hand, staring at the number on his ticket,
demanding my seat!"

Everyone gawked at the man standing
on his seat, bellowing poetry in Spanish.
Anonymous no longer,
Neruda saw the Chilean secret police
as they scrambled through the bleachers,
pointing and shouting, so the poet
jumped a guardrail to disappear
through a Fenway tunnel,
the black cap flying from his head
and spinning into centerfield.

This is true. I was there at Fenway
on August 7, 1948, even if I was born
exactly nine years later
when my father
almost named me Theodore.

THE GOOD LIAR MEETS
HIS EXECUTIONERS

—for Nelson Azócar
Valparaíso, Chile

The first time
the good liar
met his executioners
was at the military tribunal
after the coup.
Before the row of officers
withered stiff as scarecrows,
he grew more polite and forgetful
with each name tolled
on the list: *"No, señor. No, señor."*
On the wall, the portrait of General Pinochet,
mustache and sunglasses, glowering.

The good liar returned home that day,
but singers of red songs
reddened the waters of Chile
face down in the current,
and the executioners kept watch
over blazing pyramids of books,
so a passport was forged
with a plan to leave Chile by sea.
Somewhere the waves
rumbled a prayer for him
like a chorus of monks.

The second time
the good liar

met his executioners
was at the dock,
hunched in a peacoat
with a sack on his shoulder.
A pistol dug into his neck,
chamber clicked
like a bored sergeant
cracking his knuckles.
The guard disbelieved the passport
stamped Merchant Marine,
the list of names quivering
in his other hand.

"My name is not on that list,"
the good liar said,
and since his executioner
could not read
without trailing his finger slowly
across the page,
the pistol relaxed, leaving
the imprint of the barrel,
and only the passport was burned.
Somewhere the sea lions
lumbered from the foam
and waited all night for him.

The third time
the good liar
met his executioners
was at the house of his mother.
Now his name was on the list,
troops rifle-jabbing him

still in his underwear
to the pickup truck,
family on the sidewalk
begging to give him
at least the dignity of his pants,
neighbors listening with bowed heads.

On the way to the firing squad,
a balding hill where every skull
recalled the bullet's cloud of ink
flooding the brain,
the good liar invented fables
of a colonel he knew,
barbeques in the backyard
and dating his daughter,
boasting to the other
condemned compañeros
loud enough
for curious executioners to believe.
The truck circled back
and left him at the jail instead,
thirty men in a room
jostling for a peephole to breathe
or a rubber pot rocking with piss.
Somewhere the ocean boiled for him,
as if here a giant octopus had wrapped itself
around a warship full of admirals.

After bail, the good liar
smuggled himself away from Chile,
the green waves lifting him.
"You have to be a good liar," he says.

In the sanctuary of steaming coffee
he tells what he knows three times,
what the lie is,
who the liars.

AUTHOR'S NOTE: SING IN THE VOICE OF A GOD EVEN ATHEISTS CAN HEAR

The following poem is based on the experiences of Demetria Martínez, a journalist, poet and novelist. In December 1987, Ms. Martínez was prosecuted in connection with the sanctuary movement, being indicted on charges of conspiring against the United States government to smuggle "illegal aliens" into the United States; transporting "illegal aliens" into the United States; and inducing "illegal aliens" to enter the United States. The charges carried a maximum of twenty-five years in prison and $1.25 million in fines. Her poetry was used against her as evidence of her involvement. Ms. Martínez was acquitted on First Amendment grounds in August 1988.

SING IN THE VOICE OF A GOD
EVEN ATHEISTS CAN HEAR

—for Demetria Martínez
Albuquerque, New Mexico, August 1988

The prosecutor spoke "conspiracy"
as if Demetria were a mercenary
trading in helicopter gunships,
not the poet with a reporter's notebook.
The prosecutor spoke "smuggling"
as if two pregnant refugees
were bundles of heroin,
not fleeing a war of slit bellies.
The prosecutor spoke "illegal aliens"
as if El Salvador were a planet
of brown creatures with antennae,
not mestiza women dividing in birth.
The prosecutor spoke of conspiracy
to smuggle illegal aliens,
indicting the poet with a poem,
her poem for two women of El Salvador,
traveling with them by way of Juárez,
evidence abducted from her desk.

So Demetria, accused, stood in the meandering
patient line of all the accused:
accused of ducking searchlights and gunshots
on the border, crossing the river
to steal televisions from sleeping suburban dens;
accused of mopping in slow lazy rings
or letting meat burn in the spitting grease;

accused of bruising the fruit with bruised hands
picking for so many nickels paid on the bucket;
accused of the bristling knives and needles,
the slash and puncture of the tattooed arm;
accused of leering with an accent
at the cheerleaders of private high schools;
accused of causing ear infections
by jabbering en español at the bar,
or pangs in the teeth of those
who mispronounce their names;
accused of skin so brown their brains must shrink
with every promiscuous generation;
accused of kissing the welfare check twice a month
so the man with a pickup truck paying taxes
can never buy a boat;
accused of conquering territory in potter's field,
crowding cemeteries with crosses
like commuters on the subway at rush hour.

But the dead, those dead exhausted
by the drumroll of accusation,
heard the indictment of Demetria.
They knew she walked at the elbow of pariahs,
quietly singing sanctuary. So the dead opened their mouths
and began to sing, not the soprano of choirs glowing white,
but the rough-throated song of people at work
or pause from work in barrios and fields,
the heart-attack seamstress, the lettucepicker in pesticide fog,
the boy who painted murals before the bullet.
In México, her peasant ancestors
sang the corrido of Demetria the Renegade to Zapata's troops.
In El Salvador, the dead with amputated tongues

could suddenly sing, their music floating like steam.
Together they would sing in the voice of a god
even atheists can hear, even a jury across the border.

And the poet was free.

GOVERNOR WILSON OF CALIFORNIA TALKS IN HIS SLEEP

The only
aliens
we like
are the ones
on Star Trek,
'cause
they all
speak
English

HUELGA

—for César Chávez, 1927–1993

Because of that brown face,
smooth weatherbeaten soil;
because of these eyes,
ringed by rain-hungry creekbeds;
because of those peasant fingers
curling around a shovel so it became
a picket sign or a flag flying the black eagle of union;
because of that voice, speaking the word boycott
like a benediction, the word Huelga
as if the name of a god with calluses:

The red in the wine stings our eyes
with its brightness,
the grape is a circle more like the world
and less like a silver dollar.

Clemente Soto Vélez (1905–1993) was a great Puerto Rican poet and political figure. He was an important activist in the Nationalist Party, a militant organization fighting for the independence of Puerto Rico and led by Pedro Albizu Campos. Soto Vélez participated in a Nationalist assault on the Capitol building in 1932. He was also editor of a Party newspaper called *Armas (Weapons)*. Charged with seditious conspiracy, he was imprisoned from 1936 to 1940, briefly released, then imprisoned again until 1942. Following his release in 1942, he settled in New York, where he again worked as a journalist, and was a key organizer in East Harlem for Congressman Vito Marcantonio and the American Labor Party. He was recognized as a major poet with the publication of *Caballo de palo* (The Wooden Horse) in 1959; verses from that book are quoted, in translation, in the twelfth stanza ("You spelled your name Klemente with a K"). Soto Vélez would serve as mentor to countless writers and artists in New York's Puerto Rican community.

He was also my friend. My wife and I named our son after him. We introduced the two Clementes on Columbus Day, 1992. Clemente Soto Vélez died in April, 1993, and was buried in Lares, the town of his birth, which was also the site of a historic 1868 uprising against the Spanish. The following elegy was spurred by a visit to his grave in 1994.

HANDS WITHOUT IRONS
BECOME DRAGONFLIES

—for Clemente Soto Vélez
Born 1905, Lares, Puerto Rico
Died 1993, Santurce, Puerto Rico

Hands without irons become dragonflies,
red flowers rain on our hats,
subversive angels flutter like pigeons from a rooftop,
this stripped and starving earth is not a grave.

Clemente, listen to the history
before your birth. Lares, 1868:
the leaves drooping like elephant ears,
the coffee whirling gently as the danza
of unperspiring linen and lace,
the boots clicking across the plaza for church
and the hour fanning the face of the clock on the steeple,
the bar in the mouth of a straining horse
and the dark man choked with a collar of spikes
for slipping chains and fleeing into the river:
all as coins in the palm of a distant king,
all the inventory of Spain.

One night after sleep in September,
the merchants fumbled
with wire spectacles at the window
to witness the levitation of rebel machetes.
The mayor curled on the floor of his own jail,
peasants showered in wine
looted from forbidden cellars,
and slaves marveled as hands without irons

became dragonflies.
Soon the Spanish troops
would sweep through Lares
dragging the cannon's operatic mouth,
and the rebels died from yellow fever
in prison, the loudly humming darkness
of Aguadilla.

When you were born, Clemente,
beneath the vigilance of midwife mountains,
the merchants of sugar and tobacco in this country
spoke with Yankee accents; the soldiers
bellowed in English and stared at what they wanted.
Their language by law
condemned the handcuffed in the courthouse,
confusing stoic children in schoolrooms of wood.
The Protestant governor promised toilets,
sucked the sugar from the stalk, then
orchestrated flags and choirs for the battleship landing
of Theodore Roosevelt.
The President scribbled notes about the flora
and snorted at the barefoot crowds.

Your people were peasants without soil,
buried in the soil
while their hair was still black.
But in the plaza of Lares,
the muttering of fever-mad revolutionaries
brushed across your neck,
pausing in the hollow of your ear.
The ancianos, with skin like cured tobacco leaves,
remembered 1868,

taught you in hoarse conspiracy
that a machete could chop
the wrist of a landlord
easily as cane.

Hands without irons become dragonflies,
red flowers rain on our hats,
subversive angels flutter like pigeons from a rooftop,
this stripped and starving earth is not a grave.

In San Juan, his eye measuring
the imperious white pillars,
a poet from Lares
appeared at the crest of the crowd
pounding sixteen hundred hands
against the doors of the Capitol building.
A sergeant insisted on his weight
before you. Then an unknown hand,
a hand of the sixteen hundred hands,
gripped yours and left a pearl-handled revolver
in your grasp. Your aim, inches
from the sergeant's mouth,
created in him a guard dog
quivering at the cry of thunder,
created in you a poetry like ammunition.
All night you halted the cars passing
through the old city, leaning in windows
with a burnished gun,
demanding a shout of Viva Puerto Rico Libre,
payment better than paper dollars
with their portraits of kings called Presidents.
Those years, like water

plunging from an anvil-headed mountain:
Albizu in eulogy held the ashes of cremated insurgents
to the sky, and the radio banned his trembling staccato,
so you committed alchemy with ink and paper in the half-light,
words black as the sleeping shoes of laborers.

Meditations on the jailhouse ceiling:
La Princesa's crumbling skin
in the summer of accusation,
the printer in his apron
nodding to police
and newspapers confiscated in bundles.
This is the law of poets and their newspapers:
for the word "weapons," a cell with no toilet;
for the word "revolution," a door bolted in rust;
for the word "Yankee," a window blindfolded with bars;
for the words "Puerto Rico," a wall of cockroaches
too fat to kill with a fist.
Your poems became a crust
sealing your eyelids, a wet string of coughing
in your throat. In Ponce, police fired bullets
through the palms of toppling demonstrators.

After four years walking clockwise in the prison yard,
after one month on parole, the courtroom
was the chapel where a heretic was ordered to pray.
The hearing was in English. The judge was thinking, in English,
about the August temperatures in Puerto Rico
and the ceiling fan flailing overhead.
The defendant Soto Vélez learned
about Lucky Strikes and Karl Marx in prison,
but forgot which words were forbidden by parole.

Four speeches in four towns, throat raw
as a swallow of smoke from shouting.
Two more years' incarceration.
The judge remembered a photograph
from thirty years ago, Theodore Roosevelt
in a white suit and Panama hat
driving a steam shovel through the canal.
The judge did not realize then
how easily the linen wrinkles,
how the heat brings palpitations.

Hands without irons become dragonflies,
red flowers rain on our hats,
subversive angels flutter like pigeons from a rooftop,
this stripped and starving earth is not a grave.

East Harlem after the War:
the ward heelers blustered
that the Red Congressman
bought steamship tickets and welfare
for every Puerto Rican coming to East Harlem,
so they would mark their ballots with his name:
Vito Marcantonio, American Labor Party.
The ward heelers never heard you at the microphone,
Clemente, your American Labor Spanish
spreading in the sky like a flamboyán tree
split through cement, till the immigrants in the street
swore red flowers rained on their hats
and floated in the shovels of their hands.
Back in San Juan, the mayor ordered snow at Christmas
dumped on the city parks
by a squadron of bombers.

You spelled your name Klemente with a K,
conjured a new alphabet
so no one kept from school could misspell a word.
Your poems were subversive angels
born in the sky,
an insurrection of sunflowers,
a goddess of fireflies,
a hurricane of persecuted stars,
a river rising on your lover's tongue.
When children drowned in the fires
of tenement wiring,
or poets burned their intestines with alcohol
to collapse on some deserted beach
of East Harlem sidewalk, you sang the poems
till your hands cramped in their fists.

Hands without irons become dragonflies,
red flowers rain on our hats,
subversive angels flutter like pigeons from a rooftop,
this stripped and starving earth is not a grave.

The first time we saw you,
you leaned over a sick woman
in bed. You loosened the bow tie
looping your neck, pushed your sleeves
back to the elbow
and pressed two fingers,
dry and delicate as straw,
against the swollen streams
in her head, sapped the storm raining there.
We could see the lightning branch
in the blue veins behind your knuckles,

and imagined the manacles
snapped across each wrist, as if
the blockade of blood to your fingers
could asphyxiate the brain.
Later, you spoke of Puerto Rico
with an exile's music:
fluorescent creatures in the water,
the caves like great eyelids of mist,
the pulp scraped from a mango seed.

The last time we saw you,
your hair was white ash against the pillow,
though we told ourselves this was not the white
of a murdered forest, but white anemone
floating, white coral sprouting
from your forehead.
You touched the face of my infant son,
named after you, as you would touch
a lost photograph,
the book where it was hidden
many years ago.
You fed us all the communion of praise,
eyes still black and bright as volcanic glass,
though the work of breathing
exhausted you to sleep.
So you slept, mouth agape,
wheezing through bloated lungs, your hands
laced across your stomach.
We knew your hands were closing,
prayed for open palms
fluttering those subversive angels to the sky
like pigeons from a rooftop.

Hands without irons become dragonflies,
red flowers rain on our hats,
subversive angels flutter like pigeons from a rooftop,
this stripped and starving earth is not a grave.

Klemente, today we visit your island grave.
We light a candle for you in chapel
beneath a Christ executed with beggar's ribs
and knees lacerated red.
He is a Puerto Rican Christ.
In San Juan Bay, a tanker from New Jersey
bursts a black artery bubbling to the surface,
so troops along the beach
in sanitary metallic suits
scoop the oil clotted into countless bags
while helicopters scavenge from above.
Lares now is the property of the state:
the tamarindo tree
planted for independence
in the plaza
blotched and gray, a rag
tied around one branch
like a tourniquet.

At the Lares cemetery nearly a year ago,
your box sank into a hole
brimming with rainwater.
Today the grave we find is desolate clay,
parched and cracking, a plank marked M75.
He is here: burial mound 75, says the gravedigger.
So the poet who named us
suffocates in the anonymity of dirt.

This is how the bodies of dissenters disappear,
beneath oceans coated with tankers' blood,
down to the caves where their voices still drip,
as the authorities guarantee
that this stripped and starving earth is not a grave,
and no one pays the man who carves the stone.
We bury a book with you, pry red flowers
from the trees to embroider the ground,
negotiate the price and labor for a gravestone
as the child with your name races between the tombs.

Klemente, you must be more
than the fragile web of handkerchief
you left behind.
You claimed your true age
was ten thousand light-years,
promised that you would someday explode
in atoms, showering down
on us in particles beyond the spectrum
of our sight, visible only to the deities
carved into the boulders by original people
slaughtered five centuries ago.
Now a dragonfly drifts to the forehead
of a vagabond declaiming groggy rebellion
in the plaza, insect-intoxicated,
protesting his own days blindfolded with bars,
his faith louder than an infected mouth.
He says that he remembers you.
On the road to Lares, a horse without a rope
stands before the cars in glowering silence,
infuriating traffic, refusing to turn away
his enormous head. We know

what the drivers must do to pass:
shout Viva Puerto Rico Libre.

Hands without irons become dragonflies,
red flowers rain on our hats,
subversive angels flutter like pigeons from a rooftop,
this stripped and starving earth is not a grave.

Albizu Campos, Pedro: Leader of the pro-independence Nationalist Party in Puerto Rico, who was imprisoned with Clemente Soto Vélez and others in 1936, convicted of seditious conspiracy. A Harvard lawyer, Albizu spent most of three decades incarcerated.

American Labor Party: Left-wing, union-based political party of the 1930s through the 1950s.

Anciano: Elderly person.

Barrio René Cisneros: Community constructed in Managua, Nicaragua, after the Sandinista Revolution on land expropriated from the Somoza dynasty; named for a combatant killed in that revolution.

Cada puerco tiene su sabado: Expression which translates to "every pig has his Saturday," referring on one level to the slaughter of a pig, and on another level to a comeuppance.

Catalán: Language of Cataluña, a region of Spain; the reference here is to the Spanish Civil War.

Corrido: Traditional Mexican narrative song; may be journalistic or historical in nature.

Cuero: Skin of an animal; refers here to the skin of a roasted pig.

Danza: Elegant dance form characteristic of the 19th-century upper class in Puerto Rico.

Flamboyán: Tree with red blossoms, common in Puerto Rico.

Guayabera: Long embroidered shirt, common in the Caribbean.

Huelga: Strike; a word often associated with César Chávez and the United Farm Workers.

Johnson, Robert: Great Mississippi Delta blues singer and guitarist who, according to legend, was murdered by strychnine poisoning in 1938.

La Princesa: Literally, the princess; a jail in San Juan, where Clemente Soto Vélez began his incarceration in 1936.

Marcantonio, Vito: Congressman from New York in the 1930s and 40s associated with radical causes, including independence for Puerto Rico; an attorney, he represented Soto Vélez and other Nationalists.

Pinochet, General Augusto: Leader of the bloody military coup in Chile in 1973, who became dictator of that country.

Ponce: City on the southern coast of Puerto Rico, and the site of the Ponce Massacre, the killing of pro-independence marchers by police, on Palm Sunday, 1937.

Tamarindo: Tamarind tree; such a tree was planted by Albizu in the plaza of Lares to symbolize the cause of independence.

Tumbao: From tumbado (literally, "knocked down"); a rhythmic pattern for bass or conga drum.

Viva Puerto Rico Libre: Long live a free Puerto Rico; an expression associated with the movement for independence.

Wilson, Pete: Governor of California who supported the anti-immigrant ballot initiative known as Proposition 187.

Zapata, Emiliano: Famed revolutionary leader, who fought for agrarian reform and the rights of peasants in the Mexican Revolution.

Martín Espada was born in Brooklyn, New York in 1957. He is the author of four other poetry collections: *The Immigrant Iceboy's Bolero* (1982), *Trumpets from the Islands of Their Eviction* (1987), *Rebellion Is the Circle of a Lover's Hands* (1990) and *City of Coughing and Dead Radiators* (1993). He is also the editor of *Poetry Like Bread: Poets of the Political Imagination from Curbstone Press* (1994). His awards include two fellowships from the NEA, a Massachusetts Artists' Fellowship, the PEN/ Revson Fellowship, and the Paterson Poetry Prize. Many of the poems in this collection arise from his work experiences, ranging from bouncer to tenant lawyer. Espada now teaches in the Department of English at the University of Massachusetts-Amherst.